First Verses

Chanting Rhymes

Compiled by John Foster
Illustrated by Carol Thompson

Oxford University Press
Oxford   New York   Toronto

OXFORD
UNIVERSITY PRESS

Great Clarendon Street, Oxford OX2 6DP

Oxford University Press is a department of the University of Oxford.
It furthers the University's objective of excellence in research, scholarship,
and education by publishing worldwide in

Oxford New York

Athens Auckland Bangkok Bogotá Buenos Aires Cape Town
Chennai Dar es Salaam Delhi Florence Hong Kong Istanbul Karachi
Kolkata Kuala Lumpur Madrid Melbourne Mexico City Mumbai Nairobi
Paris São Paulo Shanghai Singapore Taipei Tokyo Toronto Warsaw

Oxford is a registered trade mark of Oxford University Press
in the UK and in certain other countries

This selection and arrangement © John Foster 1996
Illustrations copyright © Carol Thompson 1996
The moral rights of the author and artist have been asserted

First published 1996
9 10 8

British Library Cataloguing in publication Data available

ISBN 0 19 276143 9

Printed in China

Contents

Marty Smarty

Marty Smarty went to a party
In her jumbo jet.
After tea she jumped in the sea
And got her pants all wet.

John Foster

Mabel Murple

Mabel Murple's house was purple
So was Mabel's hair
Mabel Murple's cat was purple
Purple everywhere.

Mabel Murple's bike was purple
So were Mabel's ears
And when Mabel Murple cried
She cried terrible purple tears.

Sheree Fitch

9

Ring Around the Roses

Ring around the roses
a dozen garden hoses.
Squirt you! Squirt you!
Let's all get wet!

Stan Lee Werlin

Little Amanda Sat on a Panda

Little Amanda sat on a panda,
Eating an ice-cream cone;
The panda said, 'Ouch! I'm a bear, not a couch.
Go away, please leave me alone.'

Carolyn Graham

11

Here a Bear, There a Bear

Here a bear, there a bear.
Everywhere there's a bear.

Bears in the hallway
Bears on the stairs

Bears under tables
Bears on chairs.

Bears in the sitting-room
Watching the telly.

Bears in the dining-room
Eating jelly.

Bears in the bathroom
Having a wash.

Bears in the kitchen
Drinking squash.

Bears in the cupboards
Bears behind doors

Bears fast asleep
On the bedroom floors.

Bears here, bears there,
There are bears everywhere.

John Foster

Billy-Goat Basil

Billy-goat Basil
And Billy-goat Ben
Butted each other
Again and again.

They butted and butted
And butted all day
Until they both butted
Each other away.

Clive Webster

14

A Chubby Little Snowman

A chubby little snowman
Had a carrot nose;
Along came a rabbit
And what do you suppose?
That hungry little bunny,
Looking for his lunch,
ATE the snowman's carrot nose . . .
Nibble, nibble, CRUNCH!

Anon

crunch!

from 'Spaghetti! Spaghetti!'

Spaghetti! spaghetti!
you're wonderful stuff,
I love you, spaghetti,
I can't get enough.
You're covered with sauce
and you're sprinkled with cheese,
spaghetti! spaghetti!
oh, give me some please.

Jack Prelutsky

Pick 'N' Mix Zoo

Marshmallow monkeys,
Crocodile drops,
Red jelly elephants,
Lion lollipops.

Caramel camels,
Butterscotch bears,
Toffee hippopotamus,
Chocolate hares.

Peppermint pandas,
Candy kangaroo,
Strawberry snakes
at the Pick 'n' Mix Zoo.

Celia Warren

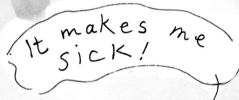

I Don't Like Custard

I don't like custard
I don't like custard

Sometimes it's lumpy
sometimes it's thick
I don't care what it's like
It always makes me sick

I don't like custard
I don't like custard

Don't want it on my pie
don't want it on my cake
don't want it on my pudding
don't want it on my plate

I don't like custard
I don't like custard

It dribbles on the table
It dribbles on the floor
It sticks on your fingers
Then it sticks to the door

I don't like custard
I don't like custard

I can't eat it slowly
I can't eat it quick
Any way I eat it
It always makes me sick

I don't like custard
I don't like custard

Michael Rosen

Monkey Tricks

Deep in the jungle
where the sun never shines,
see the Mighty Monkey
swinging on the vines.

Deep in the jungle
climbing up the trees,
see the Mighty Monkey
bend her hairy knees.

Deep in the jungle
where the tall tree grows,
see the Mighty Monkey
scratch her coconut nose.

Deep in the jungle
hear the drums beat,
see the Mighty Monkey
shake her dancing feet.

John Rice

Sing a Song of Popcorn

Sing a song of popcorn
When the snowstorms rage;
Fifty little round men
Put into a cage.
Shake them till they laugh and leap
Crowding to the top;
Watch them burst their little coats
Pop!! Pop!! Pop!!

Nancy Byrd Turner

Balloon

If you blow and blow and blow
Your balloon will grow and grow.
But if you blow and do not stop –
Your balloon will go off POP!

Barbara Ireson

POP!

Children, Children

'Children, children.'
'Yes, Papa?'
'Where have you been to?'
'Grand-mamma.'
'What did she give you?'
'Bread and jam.'
'Where is my share?'
'Up in the air.'
'How can I reach it?'
'Climb on a chair.'
'Suppose I fall?'
'I don't care.'

Traditional Caribbean

Humpty Dumpty Sat on a Chair

Humpty Dumpty sat on a chair,
Eating ripe bananas.
Where do you think he put the skins?
Down his new pyjamas!

Anon

ouch!

Listen to the Tree Bear

Listen to the tree bear
Crying in the night
Crying for his mammy
In the pale moonlight.

What will his mammy do
When she hears him cry?
She'll tuck him in a cocoa-pod
And sing a lullaby.

Traditional African

Squeezes

We love to squeeze bananas.
We love to squeeze ripe plums.
And when they are feeling sad,
We love to squeeze our mums.

Brian Patten

We are grateful for permission to include the following poems in this collection:

Sheree Fitch: 'Mabel Murple' from *Toes in My Nose,* Copyright © 1987 by Sheree Fitch, reprinted by permission of the publishers, Doubleday Canada Limited. **John Foster:** 'Marty Smarty', and 'Here a Bear', Copyright © John Foster 1996, first published in this collection by permission of the author. **Carolyn Graham:** 'Little Amanda Sat on a Panda' from *Mother Goose Jazz Chants* by Carolyn Graham, Copyright © 1995 by Oxford University Press, reprinted by permission of the publishers. **Barbara Ireson:** 'Balloon' from *Over and Over Again,* edited by Barbara Ireson and Christopher Rowe (Hutchinson), reprinted by permission of Random House UK Ltd. **Brian Patten:** 'Squeezes' from *Gargling With Jelly* by Brian Patten, Copyright © Brian Patten 1985, (first published by Viking Children's Books, 1985), reprinted by permission of Penguin Books Ltd. **Jack Prelutsky:** One verse of 'Spaghetti! Spaghetti!' from *Rainy Day Saturday* by Jack Prelutsky, Copyright © 1980 by Jack Prelutsky, reprinted by permission of Greenwillow Books, a division of William Morrow and Company, Inc. **John Rice:** 'Monkey Tricks' from *Bears Don't Like Bananas* by John Rice, Copyright © 1991, reprinted by permission of Macdonald Young Books. **Michael Rosen:** 'I Don't Like Custard', from *Never Mind* by Michael Rosen, reprinted by permission of the publishers, Longman Group Ltd. **Nancy Byrd Turner:** 'Sing a Song of Popcorn' extract from 'A Popcorn Song' in *Sing a Song of Popcorn* edited by Beatrice Schenk de Regniers *et al.* **Celia Warren:** 'Pick 'N' Mix Zoo', Copyright © Celia Warren 1996, first published in this collection by permission of the author. **Clive Webster:** 'Billy-Goat Basil', Copyright © Clive Webster 1996, first published in this collection by permission of the author. **Stan Lee Werlin:** 'Ring Around the Roses', first published in *Spider* magazine, July 1994, reprinted by permission of the author.

Despite efforts to obtain permission from all copyright holders before publication, this has not been possible in a few cases. If notified the publisher will be pleased to rectify any errors or omissions at the earliest opportunity.